by Tom Clark

Airplanes (1966)
The Sandburg (1966)
Emperor of the Animals (1967)
Bun (1968)
Stones (1969)
Air (1970)
Car Wash (1970)
Neil Young (1971)
The No Book (1971)
Green (1971)
Smack (1972)
John's Heart (1972)
Back in Boston (1972)
Blue (1974)
Chicago (1974)
Suite (1974)
At Malibu (1975)
Fan Poems (1976)
Baseball (1976)
Champagne and Baloney (1976)
35 (1976)
No Big Deal (1977)
How I Broke In (1977)
The Mutabilitie of the Englishe Lyrick (1978)
When Things Get Tough on Easy Street: Selected Poems 1963-1978
    (1978)
The World of Damon Runyon (1978)
One Last Round for The Shuffler (1979)
The Master (1979)
Who Is Sylvia? (1979)
The Great Naropa Poetry Wars (1980)
The Last Gas Station and Other Stories (1980)
The End of the Line (1980)
A Short Guide to the High Plains (1981)
Heartbreak Hotel (1981)
The Rodent Who Came To Dinner (1981)
Journey to the Ulterior (1981)
Nine Songs (1981)
Under the Fortune Palms (1982)
Dark As Day (1983)
Writer: A Life of Jack Kerouac (1984)
Paradise Resisted: Selected Poems 1978-1984 (1984)

TOM CLARK

PARADISE RESISTED

SELECTED POEMS 1978-1984

BLACK SPARROW PRESS
SANTA BARBARA ~ 1984

ACKNOWLEDGEMENTS

Some of these works first appeared in *Bachy, Beyond Baroque
Magazine, BLAST 3, Conjunctions, Credences, Harvard Magazine,
Ink, NewsArt, Ouija Madness, Poetry Comics, Poetry Now, Plough-
shares, Pulpsmith, The Rolling Stone, The St. Mark's Poetry Project
Newsletter, The Santa Barbara News & Review, Zephyr, A Short
Guide to the High Plains* (Cadmus), *The End of the Line* (Little
Caesar), *The Rodent Who Came to Dinner* (Immediate Editions),
Under the Fortune Palms (Turkey Press), and *Dark as Day*
(Smithereens).

Cover painting "Mojave Bus Station" by John Register. Reproduced
with his permission.

LIBRARY OF CONGRESS CATALOGING IN PUBLICATION DATA

Clark, Tom, 1941-
  Paradise resisted.

  1. West (U.S.)—Poetry. I. Title.
PS3553.L29P3 1984   811'.54   84-5524
ISBN 0-87685-612-1
ISBN 0-87685-613-X (lim. ed.)
ISBN 0-87685-611-3 (pbk.)

Table of Contents

Paradise Resisted: Selected Poems 1978-1984

WYOMING

Stranded in Gillette

Winter only lasts 9 months here . . . snow piles up outside
Texaco station in Gillette
bumper sticker pasted on toilet wall:

```
WYOMING IS PROUD OF ITS
OIL — COAL — URANIUM
```

All night long the coal trains rolling through
like slow, heavy executive heart attacks
Souvenir shop in Gillette
Smith & Wesson .357 mags
Ruger .44 Colt .45 on locked racks
souvenirs of life & death
lots of guys in Gillette
w/ cowboy hats, boots & limps
Rodeo injury or mining?
Osteopathic memento of booming days

Saturday afternoon
at the Center Bar, Gillette
pool table action: an intense lull
2 wildcatters vs. 2 chicks
1 Indian w/ long hair
1 in see-thru Schlitz
"Natural Lite" t-shirt
w/ bra & kinky perm like "natch'ral"

"They're so punky

they've got their flared pants turned up"

Lone cowboy drinks oblivious
tomato juice & Miller's
at quiet end of bar
on j-box W. Jennings reiterates
his belief being crazy
prevents insanity
several rounds later talk turns
optimistically to "better weather
down to West Texas this time year"

Wildcatters

Life along the Overthrust Belt is lonely. Four by fours with
rifle racks, six packs, Willie & Waylon, Miller's & a shot
can't defeat the ultimate meaning of
having to drive 200 miles in a different direction every morning
    to get to work.

Wyoming

Perhaps it's because it's such a threatening space
what with its great expanse of unaffectionate sky
that workers in this boom region travel from
job to job with their housing intact
& never further than ten feet behind them.

Robt. Smithson Would Have Loved It

Coming around a corner
to one's first vista
of a big carbon extraction scene
like the Belle Ayr Mine
in Campbell County, Wyoming
is like stumbling
into the Nile Valley
during the building of the Pyramids

Gillette

Executive class townhouses are the first thing to grow out of
the empty cliffs around Gillette since the inland sea left.
The buffalo and antelope still play amid these grasslands,
but they look a little diminished next to the Minoan scale of the
    open pit mines.

Population Control in Gillette

The coal trains go through all night long
with a racket like all of hell being unleashed as noise.
At first, as you lie in bed in your motel room or mobile home,
it merely disrupts your sleep, your nervous system. Later you kill
    your dog and wife.

Riverton

a dormitory suburb of uranus
later to receive the first
public television franchise in wyo.
but at this stage of its development still only
a wind tunnel inside which technology has allowed to nest
a small flock of mobile homes
surrounded by a good collection of
yr standard/modular rusted yamaha-impala neo-yankee junk

Uranium District in Wyoming

Driving through the yellow scorched vastness of the Gas Hills
you roll your window up tight & try not to breathe
any harder than that cow skull lying along the road is breathing.
The road curves involuntarily into the Rattlesnake Range.

Jeffrey City (I)

Jeffrey City's Downtown Air Raid Siren
creates an odd Camelotish nostalgia
U-town founded 1957, pop. 750 (1979)
JC's as old as the Quemoy/Matsu scare
a prefab frame hamlet in midst of windswept lava beds
like basecamp ville in Alaska
c.b. antennas on forlorn mobes, a brown jeep
buried ten ft. deep in filthy snow
on A St. (heart of nowhere)

Western Nuclear
Red Desert
Big Eagle

These 3 mines are Jeffrey City's *raison d'être*
if something as crazy as this place cd. be
said to exist for a Reason

Jeffrey City (II)

In Jeffrey City the snow piled up higher last winter
than anything in town except the CD sirens.
But when the sirens sounded, it was good to know
every web-hat in town could drive his house out from under it.

Neo Tibet

To come down out of the
steep colored walls of Ten Sleep Canyon
where a big game hunter from Angleterre
once fell 200 feet to his death, distracted
his fixed stare
at the sedimentary bars
                    was too intense
to come down out of that
into a terrain of bald gray domes
punctuated by
a ten foot tall bifurcate ice-tower
emitting an internal blue light
was visually too much for spectator A
who called this later: "the only time
I ever thought I was really looking at a UFO!"

Worland

Coming down out of Ten Sleep Canyon into Worland
where they still haven't cleared the dust away
from last winter's 30 foot tall drifts
which just melted down and left puddles of
everything that blew through Worland since Fall

•

That buffalo
has a lot of mud on it
and that prairie dog
acts quite neurotic
but none the less
they are not domestic yet
just nearly extinct
probably a much less silly fate.

Grasses of Wyoming and Montana

The big bluestem has roots six feet deep.
Indian grass grows with the bluestem;
switch grass also ripples there in the wind.

Going west you get less rain:
the little bluestem grows waist high, and so does
the side oats grama, & the bearded needlegrass.

Further west, the short grass of the Plains grows:
the blue grama, knee high; & the buffalo
grass, which grows up to the ankles.

S.E. Wyoming

The great trans-synaptic stack flashers
of the coal-fired electrical generating plants
that tower over the badlands across the Platte River
may provide useful power to all the Dakotas
but to the traveler they are purely retinal messengers

•

The clouds steely off over the mesas to the East
suggest twisters in the Badlands have taken away
what was owed to them by the pilgrims there
and now are moving off to test the northern settlers,
or were those twisters we saw merely the swirl above the tipples?

They won't be there to pay if they can help it.
There's no lack of character in fleeing in the teeth
of the prop wash, particularly since the new
type of technical thresher advances only in reverse.

Checking Out

Across this whole part of the continental table
Time falls away & all that's left is the dusty light of
motels in the West 30 years ago, laughter of
women somewhere off in the distance, crickets
in the violet dusk & a lonely horizontality
against which the beast shadows of the rigs are painted.

UTAH & NEVADA

In Salt Lake

All remissions are temporary
the organism will not be pardoned
whatever you can dish out
the universe will reverse
like throwing back a hand grenade
it's the boomerang translation
a dividend of evolution chez nous
barney clark in the hardware store of history
you don't win but on the other hand you lose

I Felt Sick

while watching a man
eating a ham sandwich
across the aisle
30,000 feet in the sky
over the dry lakes of Nevada
and ever since that moment
I've been seeing the animal
inside the man trying to
escape and show its teeth at
unexpected times and in
places I wish I wasn't

COLORADO

•

All I want to do
is to go
back to
Pueblo
and let the wind blow
right through me
in the parking lot
by the Trailways Depot

The Nike of Boone

In America 1980
There are many Lost Zones   sad abandoned towns
Places left behind
By the movements of commerce

One of these is Boone
A hamlet where, out among
The long rattlesnake plains
Between the Federal Train Test Center
And 400 miles of straight nothing
One is suspended out of time

And there is nothing whatsoever left to do
Except stand around that little park in
The center of town
Actually just a large patch of burnt-out grass
Where the place of honor
Usually occupied in American towns
By a statue commemorating the local war dead
Is instead taken up by a vintage Nike missile
Gay souvenir of the Days of Ike
When things were still alive in Boone

The wind blows very hard around the tall white missile
Funneling up & down the open streets of tarpaper
Shacks & broken-down mobile homes. It leans a little. It may
Blow over if the wind comes on too hard
But that's no tragedy
Nothing's no tragedy in Boone —
In fact, nothing's no nothing.

Meanings of the Plains

A volleyball game with Sam's friends the plumbers
ride out to a farmhouse off E. 75th Street where the flat land begins
96° on June 21 at 9:00 pm
heat lightning in the purple dusk & large dramatic pink cloud masses
the front range with the sun going down behind it
some kind of biting bugs no taller than a six-pack
dusty girls having trouble with their serves
coke makes an abandoned red gas pump get brighter
22 exciting volleyball games, co-educational
riding home through the buffalo grass
into the very short night

•

The first white people through here
didn't need a book to find out
the climate is, while harsh,
conducive to a sturdy temper.
You could hang a fresh stripped buffalo skin
on a line, & dry it in 24 hours
& wounds & sores closed up
almost miraculously overnight.
Fine as a pure
elixir, this air must have been
as excellent to take in c. 1800
as first class cocaine is now,
not to mention less expensive
& certainly not reserved for real estate types.

The Flatirons, Boulder

No sky is quite so blue as the
cut-out strip of cobalt canvas
they have strung up back of these
big rocks which make a spine down
the ironing board of the Plains

•

As for Boulder, the counter-drift
of westward-moving culture,
breaking up against the eastward
movement of continental weather,
splits there into the undifferentiated
social fallout of a truly rootless &
artificially created place

The Silicon Range

The flourishing on the waterless
west end of the plains
of the military, data-processing
& religious industries
shows that large amounts of
wet electronics are
no longer required by
the front line of industry
which now uses
dry chip terminals & soft displays
to reproduce &/or replace
"all ye know
or shall ever need to know"

•

High technology is mobile—with minimal
fixed investment in plant & equipment
and functions best in a high dry environment
where temperature levels are strictly fixed
inside a range that is conducive if not to the/life
of human beings, then to the behavior of silicon

Boulder

These neat little western business boys
      in the button down shirts
         they were born in—
      no wrinkles, no creases

It's the New West
         the one where
    the biggest baddest outfit
            in town
    is something called
      Storage Technology

Fort Collins

These towns all look the same
We just pass the time
punching up our favorite displays
on the video
as we pass through them

Everything's interchangeable
and as cheaply made as possible

Loveland

She's a sweet and precious thang
but when I tasted heaven
I couldn't help myself

Forgive me
I didn't mean
to do this thang

But now it's done
and my socks
are wrapped around the telephone

For my sweet thang
won't be callin'
home no more

Mountain Men

Names like Conger, Bridger, Rollins, Meeker, Berthoud
Echo through these canyons
Like summer thunder, proud and bold.
John Quincy Adams Rollins
Built the first wagon road through
The Great Divide. What didn't Sam Conger do?
A mile from here, you can call his name
And hear your voice return
Twelve times from the deepest shaft
Of the Conger mine. And you know Jim Bridger.

Men of ruthless ego all. But what of mountain ladies?
Didn't they too have pride? And what about
The narrowing ache in the bed beside
You when she wakes up to a rough face
That epitomizes 100 years of unpleasant history?

Listening to the Denver Bears in Nederland

Hats off to the first lady of Denver sports
                Mrs. Jean Harraway
and we also want to say hi
                to Steve Ratzer's wife Janet

    Harvey Barrison
            H. S. Button
                    Jack Hawley
            and Elizabeth Jones
                    out there in Castle Rock
            listening to Bears baseball

As the thunder rolls over
        all thought is crushed in its path

Eldora in July

a valley
of aspens
and wild flowers

with the wind
dithering in them

Old Mine Road (Caribou)

Just below timberline
life bursts in

where water was
it's mostly mossy

with willows
and dark spaces

and wild daisies
and mazes of glades

and pools

The Light of the World at 9000 Feet

A big
bossy-crested
blue jay
with electric black

wings
and a simonized
gorgeousness
about him

flashes into
the aspens
like sheet
lightning

Out of the Blue

Hearing my waffle soles
   crunch red rock tailings
two July-fattened

chipmunks scatter across
   the pile of junk in
the abandoned mine shaft

the sun blazes down on
   Arapahoe and Navajo Peaks
like on two ice cream cones

but nothing melts
   the air is cold
the aspens shiver

the top of the world
   isn't here, it's true
but you can see it from here

Hurricane Hill

It's nice to walk up by the old tungsten mine
But when suddenly gunfire rings out
Who has time to notice the wild flowers?

The sight of all those pockmarked tin cans
Makes wandering these slopes of aspen and pine
These meadows of columbine and Indian paint brush

A nervous pleasure

Peak to Peak

Where are the humans?
    The humans hate you so
        they went away

There are only
        the baby aspens
    whose pale green round leaves
      shimmer in the wind
    like silver dollars
            81,500 of them

1978 Coffee

In the western states
you get the great
loneliness and
sense of waste

Whereas in the
eastern states you
get the great
civilization

With either one of which
and two bucks
you can get a cup of
1978 coffee

Ben Jonson and The Bard

did gather humors of men daily wherever they came
praising sweet proportion and calling forth thundering Aeschylus
yet now their works are as out of style as 10¢ coffee
and no one has written a poem in 10 years
due to an inexorable boredom that has taken over life
for reasons we are unwilling to admit to ourselves
unless it has something to do with economics

In the IBM Parking Lot

In something as illusory as fate
Persons on earth once could perceive
If not the reasons why things happen
Then the patterns they happen in,
And perceiving these, make do.

Now there is another way, where luck is all,
And where, believing the miserable
Life we lead wasn't meant to be,
We luckily don't have to recognize
The embarrassment we are to history.

Thoughts While Watching Hodding Carter Lay Down International Law on Television

Delay is preferable to error, said Thomas Jefferson:
"Preserve your *sang froid* immovably."

Watching Hodding Carter lay down the law is like watching the
    blind umpire
Point a finger at the base thief who is clearly safe, and say "out!"

Jefferson also said, *I tremble for my country*
When I reflect that God is just.

Now America is almost grown.
It can tremble for itself.

Metaphors

Goodbye to love, life and art is on every tongue
Our time tiptoes to the edge of the extinct volcano
The future holds hands desperately with the past
The way the Flatirons look at dawn from the cemetery this
    morning
Puts death and life into a different proportion
The three big pink rocks laid out like great salmon on plates of
    snow
Down below, the ghosts of cowpunchers float up out of broken
    graves
Stroll in the air a little, legs like stiff O's, then mosey back into the
    ground
They say Hans Brinker flirted with death every minute
As he skated over the ice, yet remained stationary
And this too describes our ticklish situation

Conquering the Fear of Death

Dreams you woo me until the sun comes up then I fall
prey to many horrors not least what happens all
day long. Then I get on my bike and ride out Broadway 21
degrees and a weird crystalline hoar frost over
everything: the ugly houses on Table Mesa the
roofs of the 4 wheel drive pickup trucks full
of Nazis, they force me off onto the shoulder
I eat their dirty smoke as I swerve to avoid
the broken beer bottle climbing up hill past the
Marshall truck stop and then the road gets
steeper, crossing the long finger of one of the
mesas that wiggle down out of the Front Range.

I make my left turn on 128 toward Broomfield
the empty grass slopes move east into the rising sun
I shade my eyes with my glove and plow uphill
at the top there opens a broad field to my right
with a huge smokestack, a water tower and many
buildings where plutonium triggers are manufactured.

I get off my bike and walk over to the fence where
the sign says "Controlled Access Area" and climb over it
and walk across a field maybe 500 yards
and stop. Nobody comes to arrest me it's Sunday.
A mile ahead of me is the nuclear weapons plant.
I take off my two pairs of gloves and give the plant The
Finger. And then I walk back to the fence and climb
over it and get on my bike and ride back to Boulder.

On the way, somewhere near Superior, coming down "The
    Hump"
I hear a bang behind me and turn and see a hunter

in an Elmer Fudd hat standing on the ridge above
the road re-loading a shotgun, he is looking out to
the east, I look too, there is a perfect V
shaped flight of Canada geese moving out of his range.

A Trip to Erie

When the Chinook comes again in January and
Blows the ice floes off Baseline and Arapahoe
I ride the tract flats of the East trying to understand
The long slide show of history now almost through.

From this hill you can see the blinking signal of the laser
Beam plant in Platteville. Rocky Flats' stacks are visible.
The whole front range is perpendicular
Reality from here. It is a blinding wall

Of bad intent that hints at terrible events
By its mere propinquity. "From this rock,"
It seems to say, "will issue the burning consequence
Of a series of principles all equally idiotic."

And still in waiting for the holy
Fire to consume it, this three hundred mile long
Stretch of prairie becomes Strip City slowly
And without taste from Pueblo to Wyoming.

So is it goodbye, civilization? That's the question
These plains silently address. That, and who will care for these people
When the wind that moves across the desert like a great lion
Is all that remains of the Blue Hotel?

Life Is Great

1.

Is there any limit to the accumulation of disgrace
In a waste of shame, I guess not, well
There is no relief in quicksand here in Erie
Anyway. How to go on? By keepin' on
Keepin' on and so achieving an enormous loss of integrity.

A great noise as of a tuba comes down out
Of the mountains. A broad wave pattern hum
Follows it down the canyon. Then in
The morning light a number of Asiatics
Appear. They number in the hundreds
Of thousands. Their fingers are pointed to eternity.

2.

The blue sky is full of lions. An eagle wheels over.
There are ancient petroglyphs in the sand.
We have been dead for a thousand years.

The winged lions glory in the radiance
Of the sun. They move across the sky like great maned boats.
Their eyes are grave, clear and unendearing.

They nod slightly, knowing what we did wrong.
A painful quiet falls over the scene.
Lions never say, "I told you so."

Blizzards of Perdition

The sons of the pioneers are dying of uranium all over Wyoming,
But no one knows, and here it just snows,
Two feet, ten feet, what's the difference? In the morning
Red rocks hunch invisibly under the high blue windows
Of the sky. It is a blue of ice, not of sky,
However. Without having seen *Quintet,*
The movie, one can capture its ambience simply
By glimpsing these post-civilizational street
Scenes in which hooded, huddled figures
Shuffle through the snow in coats made out of feathers
Toward a terminal interpretation which may well be yours.

Deep Cold

Cold light and hot shade, literature clear and cold,
Cold in the earth, cold grey dawn of the morning after,
The cold breathing of one whose cold
Weeping can't be told from her wintry laughter,

Cold fruitless moon, heart grown cold in vain,
Cold empty room, heart kept in cold storage
In a cold cellar ten cold years and still unpaid,
Cold heart poured out in cold ink, burning a cold page,

Out of whose dead cold ashes life can never
Occur again, for it is fallen dead and frozen
Into a barren and remote tundra across which ever
Flee dry husks of nothing from horizon to horizon

And on this scene the cold stars look down from a cold sky
Through the frozen lens of a telescope, and cast a cold eye.

A Missing Child

Once the articulation blurs there is only
The excellent romance of the disappointment left,
And the momentum of the mind toward any anomaly
In which it is possible to locate death.

There is also the awful rowing toward infinity
In which the oars become locked
In Great Bear Lake. The snow flies
Blue and icy and fleur de lis-like

Down on the Reykjavik of the soul,
Where everything observes the quiet of the dead,
And naturally, too, the mornings grow quite cold
Ever since the sun finally departed.

A light snow fell in the night on Florida.
Mrs. Reynolds looked hard but could not find Deborah.

Murder in the Philosophy Department

No matter how much of his time Plato to his students gave
In the long winter of expendability, fresh questions filled the cave.
Asked, for example, how during battle blood mists the air
(So poets claim) as thickly as the spray made by an atomizer,
Plato replied that all existence is made of small particulars,
Including (he said) the booming surge that filled the ears
Of the people of Ecbatana, who long had left the Aegean:
Many tiny thoughts dressed up as cells imitated the ocean
In their brains, Plato explained. Then he cited Empedocles' remark to
     the king:
"The blood around men's hearts is created by their thinking,
And when this is washed away, the heart's only remaining defense
Is that no human thing is of any importance."

When the students fell back on their benches, voicing respectful oohs
     and ahs,
Plato shuffled away from the lectern, shrugging off their applause.
He returned to his dressing room very, very slowly. There
He saw four silver paper stars affixed to his door—placed by some
     prankster
Who'd received a poor grade in last term's Great Books course?
Plato studied the joke stars, then shivered. Less and less force
Seemed to pump the red corpuscles through his old veins these days.
There was no doubt about it. The best mind in all Hellas
Was slipping into silliness. But as yet no one suspected
Any of this, and he would be safe in Florida before they did.
He fumbled for the knob. The starry door swung. Through the blur
Of atoms Plato saw the plane tickets lying safely on the dresser
Where he'd left them. His heart sighed out of relief. Satisfaction
Distracted him. The shadow behind the door raised its gun.

Steve's Celestial Trained Dog Act

A chronic melancholy alternating with hysteria
Affects Steve, who has a democrat's deep fear of the Bear.
And yet, says Juan, Afghanistan is *El Vietnam de Russia.*
"It's them, not you, man, who ought to be scared."

Steve pays his taxes over and over
In his sleep, averaging out the years.
"Money equals pain divided by forever,"
Steve believes. Also, "lying equals many tears."

Who would suspect backing Steve's Celestial Dog Act
Could have made me rich—or even believe
A dog could come from heaven? Well, it didn't. The lack
Of credibility hurt us, was all that stood between Steve,

Juan, Lassie, myself and the accumulation of
A fortune. Instead, we dumbly starved for love.

Runaround Sue and Mister Kidd

On a calm sea everybody is a pilot
But this night when the waves bucked like mustangs
The young lady returned to her quarters
Where the shadows turned out to be pirates

No longer wonder at the cruelty of pirates, girl
Men may be read, as well as books, too much
Even we pirates, fascinating as we are,
Have a way of leaving you lonely nights
So shed no tears for the buccaneers

Thus spoke the dashing Mr. Kidd despite the weather
As a wind rushed in pre-emptively from outer space
It made Runaround Sue wonder about the universe
But the big ship plunged on into the night

Real Estate

She owns the soft
impeachment of her ways,
and all the rest —
her sweet smile seems to say —
is mere real estate.

Summer in the Townhouse

The pool surface is unstable
a lot of little white
plant spores
float on it
and all around it
girls oil themselves
as they read
yellow colored books
with orange lettering
partly in Tibetan

Review

Jupiter, Regulus and Mars
Appear triangulated unusually
Above the Red & White Cabins
Like heavenly evidence
That this winter's little tragedies
Are getting notices
From the big critics in the sky
But who knows their rating system?

April Blizzard, Columbia Cemetery

Snow comes down lightly as thoughts unsaid
On these plots of the forefathers of Boulder,
And as heavy as the truth of all gravity,
In a thick white spiral float
That cloaks from sight the unattended stones
Of pioneers who crossed the plains by winter
To pound these granite mountains down
Into an original state of profit
Which enables their children to move back East
And leave to nature these hard rock markers.

Only time is their caretaker now.
The pink and gray stones are chipped and broken.
Down through the moth cotton of the trees
The snow has fallen and melted against them
For six days continuously
And then fallen and drifted again
For six nights, until one imagines even the dead
Might grow impatient with the weather.

What frustrated tirades go on under this ground?
It holds, God knows, not only successful men,
Miners and bankers, but dissatisfied minds,
Vagabonds also, and outlaws ever unpacified,
Tom Horn for one. Stuck down there for good,
Does Horn still rage against his Cheyenne hangman?
Snow blows over his rose quartz stone. Time moves.
I kick the snow off and it swirls back in a white
Twister over the grave, then gently
Flutters back down like a settling of doves.

Time ought to bring solace, rest or blessing,

But in the discouragement of this age
There is a seepage into the beyond. It is a cold peace
That inches down through the half-frozen ground,
Each drip falling like a stone upon the bone.

Secrets of the Estate

Death may be the side of life's mansion
That's always been turned away from us—
But that hasn't kept us, now and then,
From sneaking around to the other side,
Where tall weeds grow over the broken statues,
And peeking in the windows.

The Problem of Anxiety (After Freud)

When the wayfarer whistles in the dark
He may be telling his timidity goodbye. Pretty smart.
We, the spectators, are impressed.
But that doesn't make him see any deeper into the forest.

The End of the Line

Two o'clock in the morning courage, I mean improvised courage,
Is what it takes to get you through this kind of night.
It lasts two years, it strikes fear across the continent,
The end is not in sight.

Oh, the end *was* in sight, but
Before my eyes
The finish line turned into a tightrope,
And then the tightrope turned into a noose.

The noose was a mile around.
But then one has an awfully large cranium.

Goodbye rhythm, goodbye rhyme,
Talk to you another time.

When you get past the capacity to react
What you get to
Is the end of the line.

After the Slide

After the Flagstaff slide
The grass grows up out of the
Asphalt like brush strokes by Memling

The great trees bow in the air
The brilliant horizontal light
Catches the bending branches from underneath
And breathes their bright greens
Into the blue violent air

From behind the first snowy peaks
There comes a kind of
Groaning noise like something large awakening

A wild Art Deco bird
The size of a catcher's mitt
Flaps up out of the red rocks
It moves its wings so fast
It seems they will come unhinged

When the wind blows this strong
The emeralds shift positions on the trees
In a kind of rotary floating drift
That creates shadows of great meaning
And dark impermanence

They say places sometimes speak to you most deeply
Just when you are about to leave them

They also say audacity wins the wars
The corollary of which is
When you lose your nerve
It's time to make yourself scarce

In Left Hand Canyon

You were wearing your arrival suit that day
It was a sight to turn one's head up to the sky
Where the Crab bingled to center for one station
It seemed like the beginning of a raging time
Light spread like a butter patty across the mesas
While the sun rose like a heated metal coil
Flung-up with skill by a starboard flinger
Into a wall of such brightly reflecting rocks
That their face, tilted to the West, received
The sun of afternoon in phases of altering
Color so deep it went into the roots of Hue.
This being true, why didn't we linger? You so wise,
Reminded me we hadn't yet arrived.

NEW MEXICO

Following Rivers into the Night

I guess it's because
the only things left in this West
I can have any real
respect for
are beauty of character
and beauty of nature

and you know the two
breed one another
in those long miles where
there is nothing to do
as the sun goes down
over the flat horizon
but watch it gold-ify
the surfaces of rivers
from the Belle Fourche
(or Foosh, as the locals say)
to the Cimarron
which will push on into
the darkness with its light
flickering over them like a skin.

War

The desert moves like a museum made out of light.
Its mighty magnitude goes on and on.
It blasts the sleeping woman in her bed. It
Blasts the sleeping man. They are made clean.
Then the wind moves off to Afghanistan.

These are millennial figures.
The tank sits upon the white sand.
The men are away from home for the first time.
Beyond them the great lonely peaks glisten.
They will hear familiar songs in the night wind.

Over to the east the great fires will burn
And burn. Something moves restlessly along the sand.
The wind picks it up and blows it away over the desert.

It is gone into another dimension.
It is like a memory or an artifact in a museum.
The desert washes everything clean.
A bright dog runs from Kabul to Albuquerque.

Billboard Mirage

Throaty aggressive garble
of spoken Navajo
is only thing truck radio
picks up
as we pass down
the main drag
of Gallup, New Mexico

An oil boomtown now
Haven't been thru here
for 30 years — once
a one horse stop on 66

Still the same big yellow
sandstone buttes
to the north   ghastly under the desert moon

A werewolf
passing through here
in the dark
on the way down to
Nogales
wraps his fur tight &
looks both ways
before dashing across
the highway

The long desert
stretches out in front of us
@ 110 degrees
a billboard mirage
precariously wavering
out of which

The scorched light
of automotive america
rushes from east to west
like air blowing out
of a suddenly opened blast furnace

The pressure of the future
may or may not
burst out into space
but this much I know
At the truck weighing station on US 40
the state of the nation
is dry shakes
& a dusty choking nausea

A little high plains nihilism
in the lost emptiness
of the great Southwest
is perfectly appropriate
as is that cactus
over by that rock

What I mean to say
is naturally distorted
by the line noise of memory
but if I drift here
another year or 2
I hope to clear that out also

Then perhaps I can show you how
the feeling of passing through
has been fastened down in very
few places on the planet
as perfectly as here

ARIZONA

•

Even the sun, striking our eyes
so blinding & frontal
all across Arizona
was there to tell us

>not to cross over
>the state line

This becomes part of the
old slow story of the West
that begins when the
first snow falls

>and ends when
>the visitors depart

What the Pioneers Always Wanted to Do Was Arrive

Which meant getting across the mountains alive
but then what? You lost track of the lessons
of the journey when the beginning fell out of sight
beyond the black unreeling truck lane of eternity

Out the window it helps to sing, Goodbye
to the pronghorn, & the buffalo
drops his shaggy head into the unreclaimed sage
unremarking our mechanized passage

Who at the end, may come to tread
the thick lawns of the Biltmore
which unravel from bungalow
to bungalow, trued perfectly
as strips of crushed money
leading into infinity

Standing on them, it will be possible
to look back to the east
and truly see nothing
of what we have crossed over
for the first time

CALIFORNIA

So Cal

Here if anywhere else in America, I seem to hear
the coming footsteps of the Muses.
                                    — W. B. Yeats

Those who came from places
that produced corn, wheat, butter & eggs
to a place that produces celluloid images, computer chips,
drive-in taco stands & aerospace components
have never stopped wondering, "What am
I doing here?" They believe some destiny awaits the place.
They believe this because somebody told them so.
It's a belief that's really a lot more like a feeling.
They can't remember who it was that sold them
all those neon poems
you hear echoing through this cathedral of empty
headed intentions they call home. The only false
note here is my referring to them as "they."

Trouble in Paradise

I didn't come here to
milk your sacred cow
or even to
slaughter her

As a matter of fact
the first time
I looked at her crosswise
she turned into goat cheese

The Rodent Who Came to Dinner

They say this part of California
Is paradise on earth for the roof rat,
Who loves the palms & vines of the middle classes,
The ubiquitous fruits, the delectable nuts & ivy.

Just another genus struggling to become indigenous,
When it arrives they switch the menus. But it won't leave.*

---

* cf. the medfly

The Nelsons in SR

Those bungalows of San Roque
so perfect yet oddly sad
("a little wood & stucco
to keep the sun out")
always remind me of
where the Nelson family lived
way back in the days of Hi Oz
Hi Pop Hi Rick Hi David.

Everybody in that family was Okay
every day for a whole decade.
And when Ricky turned out to be
a low rider, it was still okay.
And that's the way it is today
among the petticoat palms
of Calle Noguera
and Puesta del Sol.

You can't rain on the parade
of the petit bourgeois
because it doesn't have one.

●

They say San Roque
is only one step
away from heaven

but keep in mind
that could be a
step in the wrong direction

Short Bats

Everybody here is good at what they do
Which is, in most cases, Nothing

"Laid Back"

Cecil Rhodes
wd. have liked it here
excellent climate
plenty of nat. resources
high prop. value
& natives nearly as totally subdued
(&/or supine)
as their favorite catchphrase indicates

A Last Squint at the Beach Volleyball Finals

This scene evokes (if anything)
viet nam, where the body
count was all that showed
whereas here, the body
show is all that counts

jane fonda has a scrawny ass

I've been in the lower class and the middle class
those two were enough for me and that's why
I don't want to join the exercise class

Things to Do in California (1980)

Play beach volleyball
Make surfboards & live at Dana Pt.
Pick up chicks galore
Shine it on & get a good suntan
Catch cancer from the chemicals in the water
Die a grotesque death
Have a movie made about your life
Make sure you look thin in every scene

Priests of Newport, Manhattan & Laguna

The soi-disant "arrested and/or automated
adolescent," a market analyst unmarked by 29 autumns,
goes to the wet bar in his Baal Beach condominium
and blends a potent combination
of limeade, rum and ice cold yogurt

"Time to get happy," he tells us,
as he gets ready to go out into the Babylonian noon
& kick sand in somebody's face
with a foot that's a nearly perfect prosthesis
from suntanned tendons to golden fat of calf

The Class Doesn't Struggle Anymore

Why is it so unsurprising that
the little man in the white coat
who drives the small motorized cart
across the manicured putting green
that grows like crushed money
between the bungalows of the Biltmore
doesn't appear to enjoy the acquaintance
of the thin old man in the italian sweater
who emerges from one of the bungalows
tugged along by a tiny expensive dog?

All Television Is Real

Hey, it's Christmas
let's break out the canned fruit
& put through a call
to yr. mother in Santa Maria

She makes the best tuna sandwiches
I have ever tasted
and did you ever notice
how much better they taste under fluorescent light?

But if she serves them
again this year on the holiday
I promise you this much
I will share them with you

because you have shared
everything with me, even the packages
of candy bars and antibiotics
you stole from the americanos' factory

●

The lost hard "g" in Los Angeles
a consonantal position swept away like all else
in the great laissez faire flood
from Chula Vista to Los Olivos
Jack Webb said it as
"Los Ang-less"

So did my grandfather, who liked it here

Nowadays though, they say it soft
without much meaning
to change it, but changing it
all the same—like taking the "O"
out of "Adios," and putting it back in "Idiot"

Or like the big developer in tartan plaids
who says to the local don of Zoning
Buon giorno! on a beautiful morning
before they divvy up the rights to the aqua
for another patch of the sun-deluged townhouses
that stretch from here to Solvang
in an unraveling irregular torus like an orange
peeled by an unsteady celestial hand

Oaks & Entropy

The antique oak *sobre la veranda*
has to lean on one elbow
to exist: but so does almost
everything here. At least the tree has
an excuse, it is over a
hundred years old. But still grows slowly . . .
here, in Ojai, in Paso Robles,
the shade it creates is noble, artful
and especially in the afternoons
gives the gardens a light-checkered
repose that is shapely and not torpid.

So select this land.
No wonder the Spanish stopped.

So select these ocean-lying hills,
bowers of lemons and oranges, and
old oaks thickening and making
the land cohere around themselves.
It's a coherence that's proudly
undemanding of water or attention;
as personable as shade, or good
conversation; rooted, firm
and dry-leaved, with beams
that leak through to the foundations
like quick sun rays.

So select this land.
No wonder the Spanish stopped.
No wonder the professionals
supplanted them. Dying
painlessly over years can

107

be a way of life;
it can provide meanwhile
and nobly for everything around it,
like the oaks do and did;
or it can use everything up
and disappear into the end
of history, without taste or care,
a style that's much more modern.

Into

the great live-oaks, dense of
limb & leaf, that once
mantled these valleys
with a solid green
"through which
one could ride
for miles in almost
perpetual shade,"
James Dean gunned
his Maserati, Gucci'd
foot to floor, sense of
balance tied
to a badly frayed
interior time clock
over which destiny
crept up by the minute,
his scarf blowing
back into the
disappearing sunbeam

Another Exotic Introduction, Revised

Nothing but psychodrama
& disillusionment
in the canyons of the wealthy

Still there's a swell sunrise
up Gibraltar Road a ways
where the red-yellow spectra
of the rising sun to the left (east)
get up above the marine layer
down around Ventura County
and all Montecito's
hazed terrarial shadows erupt at once

The resultant sky is a story
of wild peach liqueur
spilled on dirty pillows

South Coast Flora

In the face of all these
exotic introductions
like all forms of the petticoat palm
with its little white flowers on top
shaped like dollar signs
the native coastal shrub & chaparral
is made to Stand Back
as is anything native anywhere
in the swirling movement or onslaught
of small arrested dunes
of floating capital

South Coast Epistemology

The meaning of objects in
the desert is great
but here, where everything
is grown-over
with human clusters
nothing is clear
everything is shifting,
constructed
& merely apparent

The Pack Approaches the Mission

The sun dies into pink smog off Goleta
& over toward Point Concepcion
the violet reptiles of the night
begin to slide across the sky
like pieces of neon tubing.
In such lighting the wild dogs
are held momentarily at bay.

The building blocks of a superior logic
seem to slip into place
with a quiet authority. The moon comes up.
There is a small click. It is evening.

It is of course the
evening of the very rich
who do not like to lean
into the wind. They stand, the pair
beyond the camphor tree on Laguna Street
bathing in its fragrance. Two old dames.
Perhaps they are not very rich after all.
It may be just the blue hair that fooled me.

It may have been the failing light.
It may have been the falling rose-colored
flowers of the pink flame tree,
or pieces of their pods,
which are covered with rusty wool,
that fell through the air
and affected my vision.

It may have been the pollen in the air,
the fluffy cotton heads which have

just burst from the floss-silk trees,
or floating strands of the dark
hair-like fibers that are
shed by the fortune palms
whenever the breeze arises.

There is a serenity about this apparition
but it is abruptly broken
by the peremptory bark of the pack-leader,
who, poised at the brink of the trees, signals
with a crazed snarl for the rest of the pack to advance.

Dear Doctor

A rat swam toward me
in my hot tub

I shut my eyes
and took my b.p.
by bio-feedback

& outside I heard
the random snarling
of the packs

Collaborators

There are people so sick
in Lynwood, Downey,
Paramount & Hawthorne
as to leave out
paper plates of food
in alleys
to keep the wild dogs alive.

Poet as Wild Dog

In the unbuilt freeway corridors of L.A.
"man" has provided
a perfect environment for
the wild dog. This is why

I call these streets home,
these canyons of concrete
in which I hope to evolve
bark by angry bark

into a new art form
truly representative
of the 21st century.

Under the Fortune Palms

Some people think meanings are hard to find
In the 1980s decade of great emptiness
Among the bungalows of Samarkand
I stood under the fortune palms
And watched for a sign to blow by
In the throbbing Santa Ana
But all that came my way
Was the remote echo of a woman's voice
From down around Xanadu Street
Calling for her dog to stay

Off Goleta

Suddenly on the Mission lawn
A guy tosses a frisbee catching sun glints
Into the vermilion jaws of dusk
While above the frayed palms
A great sherry party takes place in the western sky
With catering by Giambattista Tiepolo
Eternity is in that moment
As if the sun were going down over Venice
— And there one stood, *maestro di pintore,*
Calculating the finishing touches —
Instead of only off Goleta

•

Halloween on the south coast
red bugles break into
ceruleans & manganese blues
the white blossoms of the yucca
pasted against absolute cobalt
the salmon pink of the Santa Ynez
deep palm greens & straw ochres
cobweb greys of the pines
the silver dollar turnover
of eucalyptus in the slipstream
northeast wind chases the aerosols
off & brings in all these colors

Pacific Melt

Wild form, deep form, form out of the
                                    Arabic night
God, your conspicuous discrete
desert stars are trucks of light
on very distant highway 101's
                                    over which
I am hitchhiking tonight

The waves feathering out in ink
beyond Obispo, toward Concepcion
toward Surf, a black like blue
jello out of Jules Verne star-bowls

the world a crushed grape to
someone on Betelgeuse

Stoicism Now

Qualifying by my powerlessness for a life
of following the air currents that blow down
the corridors of the Labyrinth of Lost Angles
which are like the sub-grandstand on the other
side of the walk-through mirror in *Orphée*
I find that midway through the whole journey
my fatalistic noir ethos disappears & is
replaced by a sense of being a dull weak guy
impecuniously pumping gas for a living
on a lonely high desert where no cars pass
I was given a long term contract on this job
The kind where they don't pay any royalties
There's nothing to do but watch the rats
run around the pump in the dawn's pink oxymorons

Winning the Kewpie Doll Made of Platinum, I Slip on the Mirror Bringing It Home to You

The elegance of the 2-bit hustler
who pulled off a dangerous caper
keeping a rendezvous with Dr. Snuff
all to win a silver star
with which to decorate the night sky—
his whole collection pasted there
on the ceiling
of the cold bedroom of his lover—
is very probably spurious
Nevertheless the struggle toward freedom—
O fallen angel of the moon
whose passions fill my notebook
of foolish behaviors—
is one I will act out forever

Biological Supremacy

Biology still reigns supreme
In this zone around your hips
Where perception guides me
To perform what is no more than
The expected function after all
But let one thing be understood
I'd be dead if it wasn't for
The inspiration provided by your body
By which I don't mean information
For there are some things one can't know
They are of course the only things worth knowing
And it is the pursuit of these
On an everyday basis no less
Which makes life almost worth living

Why We Need a New Ballad Mode

What's simple
joy division
in the beginning
later makes
every little cell
wring its hands
and bang its head
against the bulkheads
of its being

that's why love
can't be trusted

Whatever Happened to Don Ho

I used to watch Hawaii Five Oh
in Bolinas
but not on television
it used to cross
the northwestern sky
in yellow thunder strikes
making tiger violets
stripe the early nights
which were so wet and deep
you could love and live and
let live in your little GTO
and I could drift out back
and drop my sleepy sack
amid the plants
and play "easy street"
on the 12 string
I never thought your flesh wd wither
whether or not
history came to pass and I never
thought we wd enter Time
I had a good reason
for taking the easy
day trip into skyfulness
night after night
it took me so long to find out
but I found out
so here I am lost in the present again
forgotten but not gone
with an imaginary ukulele on my knee
and a wide grin only in my
don ho imitation I dont do for you anymore

Egyptology

So it's a desperate exile cold desert light that flees
The salmon pink of the Santa Ynez at 5:52 AM in November
Color with power to make men forget slow exile days
Knowledge w/o power to move, light moves in no trees
Men stand around dying in the deserted Sierra Madre
What else is there to do? Horses die too, also camels
Overcome by quiet of Egypt, the sense of inspissate gloom
All this air, all these clouds
That go down with Moses into a cadmium
Dawn exploding in soaring stages over the bullrushes

•

Over the Santa Barbara Racquet Club
Like a gold tennis ball dandled on a gas jet
The sun bounces up into the sky.

On those courts the most beautiful women
In the world rub eau de cologne into their round legs
And then leap like springboks at passing-shots,
Gulping in vitamins of light out of the burning blue.

They get up this early to play because of fires from within.
They give their utmost up and on.
The fires smolder.
The story is always old and always new.
If I tell it to you here, it is only because it is what
                                they have said first with their bodies,

Bodies which may burst into flame at any moment.

•

I stand
on my pedals
racing down Foothill above
      the Tennis Club

Where there is no
    caring
            there is no feeling
                — but then
from the deep crevasse below me
    there arises
a broken emotional cry
    "Forty-love!"

Little Elegy for Bob Marley (d. 5/11/81)

I turn the bike home thru the freeway haze at Rincon
Heading west into the flow of the commuter pack
It's rather hard to concentrate thru this fog of mistrust
This aerosol inflected loss of perspective
It's probably meant to serve as a relief from history
But history still has a way of stating its case
As when the evil snail wraps itself around the sad faced
Singer-saint's spinal stem & wrings out the last of his existence

Valley in Relief

The frightening ballast of dust licks
The sky that fades from lavender to beige
The red tips of the bougainvillea are
Lit by some kind of internal gas
Also legible on maps of purgatory

An unfolding topology of tracks
Over which
Cars move between the flat dark areas
Through the
Motionless light diffusing haze

Dear Customer

Quit your gripes about the bad air
being the dead end
of civilization as known

According to Rédiffusion du Sud
it's only a serious case
of dissolution by aerosols
in Le Cimetière Tropique
where invisible particles corrode
the anti-frontiers
and leak a desert music
into the marine band

An advancing state
(in other words)
of post-Club Med tristesse
expressed thru the business end
of a Porsche exhaust pipe

More Crooked Lines from Paradise

If you've got a problem, come on over
It's like heaven up here
but you can get lost in the likeness
fumbling in a wet similitude through
too many consecutive turquoise days
tiptoeing around the corrals of the rich
leading up to the brink of the autopsy
sometimes it almost makes you wish
you hadn't died, so you couldn't dig all this

A Polyester Notion

We have reached the other side of the harbor
the sails of the yachts are slapped against the sky
like acrylic colors straight out of the tube
equally thoughtless and simple is the deep
lavender backdrop against which the ochre
mountains are flatly & theatrically stacked

We can keep on continuing along this line
as far as the grave of Ronald Colman or we
can double back and visit Ross Macdonald's
locker at the swim club though I seriously doubt
Robert Mitchum will be there what with
the polo season opening this week & all that

Lines Composed at Hope Ranch

Twist away the gates of steel
— Devo

O wide blossom-splashed private drives
Along which sullen mouthed little guys
In motorized surreys
Ride shotgun over spectacular philodendra!
O paradise of zombies!
O terminal antipathy to twist
And shout!
O hotel sized garages
Inside which smoothly tooled imported motors
Purr like big pussies under long polished hoods!
O fair haven of killjoys
United to keep surfers off
One of the great beach breaks
Of the West Coast!
O floral porticos, flowers
Of de Kooning, de Chirico
Chateaux! Estates where jokes
Aren't funny! What secret meaning waits
Behind your stone & steel gates
Your walls of bougainvillea
Your date palm lined roads
Your quiet oak shaded lake
Like a European protectorate in Tanganyika?
Surely nothing disorderly, nothing disarrayed
Nothing at all except the great Pacific swell
Of money!

At the Rita Hayworth Surfboard Bar 'N Grill

A pointed tin roof
cute wood shingles
stuffed macaws
revolving ceiling fans
banana trees
birds of paradise
pineapple daiquiris
bamboo swizzle sticks
sarongs soaked in lizard spit
sigh
I'm starting to think
maybe Tiki's too tacky
even for me

Election Day in Sleepy Mission

Life should have enough arresting moments
to create at least a tropism in Xanadu

but little is expected by those who
live in the environs of the lawn bowling court

for them it is a perennial Mondo Samarkanda
and Reagan now coming home to roost

in their sunset is like the great snork bird
of Papua homing in on orange juice

A Brief Review of FREE TO CHOOSE
by Rose & Milton Friedman

The fact that
the logical conclusion
of Milton Friedman economics
as donated to Chile
is an economic situation wherein
unemployment in the shantytowns
is 100% among males
and when the military moves in
to halt protests staged behind
jerrybuilt barriers of burning tires
the protestors are forced
to sit naked on the burning rubber
certainly doesn't prevent
the young businessmen and -women
at the santa barbara ymca
from the ad nauseam quoting of Rose and Milton
between muscular laps

Resignation

While Jim Watt on the Barrack ranch
rides a red horse off into
the alizarin sunset of el nino
(grinning "thank you" before he goes)
traces of the oil he consigned to lease
percolate up through the layers
onto the white beaches of isla vista
to stick to feet of rich kids from orange
county. No protests here today,
only surfboards, frisbees and high interest
passbook/checking @ the BOA.

In a Vacuum, a Single Emission Can Become Smog

This part of the country is definitely a
corner pocket when it comes to word
music. For instance although he's
got a tin ear over there under the palm
trees and Nazi architecture of Cal Tech
the only poet/editor in SoCal who can fit
an entire cantaloupe in his mouth
without opening his lips
is being interviewed by the L.A. Times
as a force in the Arts
because of his new magazine named after farts
featuring the works of Mr. Dull and Mr. Slack,
snores in front and snoozes in the back.

The L.A. Times makes sure
to get all this straight so tomorrow
morning out there under the rat cluttered palm trees
of Nowhere, the suckers & hustlers & dilettantes
can lap it up. And when they do,
it will thereby become The Culture.

The Decline of Western Civilization

darby crash & the mint jelly
as far west* as civilization
as known can come and still
have a pet tarantula

----

* The direction denoting also a
movement *outward* into vertical space
and/or *the* entropic/evolutionary move
of the '80s = the brain has been blown
out through the top of the head
(cf. *Alien*) somewhere in the not too
distant past (going west no doubt)
and leaves behind this fossil form of
a once "rational" species ("Manimal").

A New Twist Is All You Can Expect in the City of Angles— A Poem wherein: an Heir apparent appears like an apparition in the unapparent air (but is deposed by lithium and history)

Out of the lies, out of the wasted
post-industrial freeway blight
Out of the broken glass, orange
skies and white grit of the image
capital of the universe, where tongues
of sensation loll idly in young mouths
like forgotten vowels for cities Atlantis
could never match for loss; out of dull
orgies and stoned idylls enacted
with half-hearted passion in hideaways
of Silver Lake, Echo Park and Venice;
Out of burning gazes ever aspiring
to the billboard glitter of a Hollywood
which is less visible than the
nitrous moon; out of a stardust-
stunned, vinyl-blinded imagination whose
hyperbolic bravado aches carefully in
the missing romantic moonlight; out
of the slack, affected grief of a
studio werewolf with a black spandex
stocking pulled over his head, who can't
find his way home to the pinned,
mascara'd eyes of the eighteen year
old runaway awaiting in the day
bed of a wooden bungalow, so who-cares,
under a light like solid lithium,
so new wave, so cocaine; out of the whole
blank seriousness so depeche mode, so
sullen-modern, so essentially *light*

emerges *this* latest white hope
for a future literate culture, twitching
with small premeditated seizures,
posturing against history from minute
to minute, even as the smog-charged
limelight shifts, & culling
the worst awards of a dead society
like a 2-bit imitation of Yeats' rough beast
as it skulks toward New York to be borne.

The Muses' Exodus

Out of the fading morning fog, in a powdery blue day
under the bays of the oak and the laurel
one can almost imagine the soft forms moving

to a hype that insinuates like music from a zither
deep there, out of the rocks, by the spring
where the oracle waits with lips pressed
almost as tight as the drawer of the cashbox

Free Lance

The quest for winter sunshine washes
The gasping survivor up on the shore
Much that's done isn't meant
Much that's meant isn't done
I take it up & at the beck & call
Of some remote agency I stick it in
& when it's over I pull it out again
Like the bloody *assegai* of a born liar
Every wave lines up behind the last one
The days wash away the days
The waves wash away the shore

•

I drift, out of reach of infinite Idiot Monkeys
who wrote the Life Script as a joke for money
(these are the writer-monkeys of the cosmic
Tonight Show etched on my brain by dreams), and yet
not really out of their reach

                    A Mondo Tremendo
beckons from beyond the benign mask of fog
but vanishes too swiftly into a policy
of scorched earth pursued from the mundum tremendum
not yet visited by the magellans of atari
who took six thousand years to discriminate "X"

Pilot to Terminal

Light in a box came too late to rescue
Temporary booty of the wet plasm splitting
Divided up into the dry greed of offspring
It grew hungry to exist at whatever cost
And to encourage this, on the Sony in the cellblock,
Something sings from Tokyo to Ossining
And what it sings is Hold still and devolve
The animal's last gasp is simply the beginning
Of life in the machine whose singer's a chip
Honed like an atoll till cutting edge distribute
Translucent surface into phosphorescent husks
Which float on soft waves across that calm bay
Of retinal assent, where crystal blue persuasion
Sucks all thought into an undertow-like coma

The Clash

One hard act of cognition
can put the whole
system
       outa commission!

"Gotta lose this
skin I'm imprisoned in"
all right, but that
still leaves the burning
question of the meat
strung across the bones
inside the skin

The New Thing I Told Myself on Olive Street

yesterday was another one
of the last days left on earth
but who's counting this string
of pearls? who'd want to
those my thoughts as I hobbled
trying out my homemade shoes again
in the new valley of dolls down
canon perdido street way
where in this gray a.m.
the men are already lined up
outside the state assistance office
with (at this late date)
not even the appearance of
false cheerfulness left
So I make it around the corner
there's a guy lying face up
to the sky on city sidewalk
wino I guess with bottle
in paper bag only out like
a light or some dead amigo
on slab in city morgue
"Don't be afraid" I told
myself afterward limping
away "to go down
deep and blow upwards
from there, to the Lord,
like a diver in shit ocean . . ."
talking to myself these days . . .
"Reach down
        to your toes and know
and know
how deep it goes . . ."

kinda humming it
"down past the pink notes
to where they get blue
outa squids". . . I crossed Carrillo. . .
"nobody down there know your name
nobody down there know you
and you know the real sound
you get (that moan)
is the one you pull out of
looking up at the bottom
all the time, anyhow besides"

but it didn't help

I'll Say Yes to the Ocean

Because it won't accept my no any more
I'll ray out into the day
But I won't say the sayless sentences
The boats will sail into the soft
White spray making their way out
Past the drill rigs' spidery struts
To the blank horizon becoming gray-
On-white dots like aces of snow
Fading away into Pacific February
Out there where the current pulls
Beneath the flat cold slate blue
Voicing a certain I don't know what
That down deep has so strong a draw
Nothing lost to it ever surfaces
Before I fall I'll look below
I'll know what I have to know
It'll be a knowledge like the hole in a donut

Twenty-one guns
and a snorkel
won't get you through heaven's
gates of coral
I mean you can
swim out as deep as you like
toot your salute
with no matter how many
sweet & graceful notes
into the breeze marine

Here come the dark fins
cutting across the water

Under the Young

The young sharks feed peaceably in the shallow waters.
Because they are strong and proud, they get a chance to be silly.
The old sharks move out to the deeps, hungry, restless and driven.
They are only serious.

Kenneth Patchen

"Apply another time?
Are you trying to be
the Kenneth Patchen
of your generation?"

That was my wife
implying
I ought to give up

Kenneth Patchen
            never gave up
and that's how I want to be
obnoxious, aggressive
out of it but at least not
part of the twilight
of the idiots

Stooges Anonymous

You see us as ridiculous and you laugh
We don't care if you laugh
We'd laugh too

We are a miscellaneous class
Our backgrounds are diverse
The things we do are various
But here is what unites us
We only act this way for cash

We are Stooges Anonymous
We lower ourselves for money
You may humiliate us
You may embarrass us
You may do anything
You want to us
Because we are
Stooges Anonymous!

We're educated but we got no ideas
No standards No beliefs No class
Speaking strictly we're trash
Speaking any way at all
We're still trash
Got no manners No personalities
We're stooges
Stooges Anonymous
We do it for cash

We lower ourselves for money
We do any kind of act
You may think we're pathetic

You're right we say
Just don't try telling us
The check's in the mail

Manifesto: Anti-Performance

I give everybody a pain in the ass
Myself included
Elevating mere difficulty
Into a form so pervasive
As to surround myself with executioners
Just to satisfy a sense of humor
So low it assumes you have
To be a little bit dead
To be really funny

Thus without becoming dull
I am rendered very tiresome
In a deliberate auto-da-fé
Conducted under a guise
Of soliciting the resentment of those
Whom I consider disgusting
A process excessive in all respects

Yet when asked to perform
As the geek of my own convictions
I demur on grounds
I won't hurt myself for you
I've done that already—too many times
I'll just stand up here
And let you see the effects

To write is to mutilate the soul
It's not a sideshow
It's not a performing art
Here is a picture of the writer performing:
Ugly man lost in thought
Invisibly cuts out chunks of his own heart

Sucks on the end of a pencil
We fall asleep watching him . . .
Snore!
Yawn!

la chanson du mal pensé

I'm ending up even worse than I started
the way I started out was not so hot
I've never really known what I was doing
one thing I've never had is personal charm
you have to have that to get ahead

born in Chicago nineteen and forty one
forty three years later I've still got
a lot of Chicago in my soul but
this is one time and place where you
might as well have a soul full of tacks

what you need now is a soul full of helium
or any other lighter than air gas
on second thought you might do
better not to have any soul at all
if you want to get a leg up on those

morons out there they have a similar
lack that's their advantage in fact
it's the age of the triumph of the mediocre
if you disagree it's because it's hard to
think clearly with a brain full of helium

or any other lighter than air gas
of course there's always the temptation
to blame all this on the idiots who drive
around on freeways on network tv
shows but they aren't really to blame

when society goes bad it's the artists
who are at fault it's their responsibility

to keep things always honest and alert
and when they begin to lie to themselves
and each other the whole culture goes soft

it's because the train of thought
has forever left the station
the train with the thought of artists
on board which is supposed to move
through the towns puffing fresh air

no one knows how to catch up with it
everybody looks around but all they find
is the fast distraction of cash
and carry aesthetics which reward
mediocrity with an instant grant

and you walk around or stagger
as best you can and your lungs fill up
with bad stuff and you get dizzy
and can't stand up and when you reach
for something to support you

there's really nothing there any more
nothing solid enough to hold on to
only the spreading intoxication of lies
which move directly from the mouth
to the brain like an infusion of helium

or any other lighter than air gas

January down the Canyon

Wind scythes the night like a biopsy of time.
I see in postoperative dreams
icy tranquilities, the calm, possessed
eyes of laboratory animals,
which show their time is come, yet never waver
because they no longer close. Paralyzed
is one step past numb.
                              All night the Santa
Ana thunders down Mission
Canyon. Something tumbles from the sky
onto the roof. The house shakes, wild
starlight shakes the venetian blinds,
excited roof rats race terrified
out of the yucca, chittering
in that strange trebly roof rat voice
as if a terrible beauty can't be borne
without a simultaneous high
anxiety. Eyes frozen
open stare at nothing in the dark.
I get up and fumble for the codeine.
Every minute we choose to die
or live. But is this dream of life a choice?

R.I.P.

I know a man
who complains and suffers
too much
were it permitted
to inventorize them for you
in all their totemic
and secret particulars
I'd itemize his pains
but paradise resisted
reduced to specifics
produces merely lists
of individual tears
too trivial for literature
say simply
instead, if
to exist is human
to forget's divine; and
a man is closest
to the image of a god
when his memory
is touched by
the time eraser

Those men whom the gods wish
to destroy, they first make
mad, and then, when the first white flecks
of foam speckle the men's lips—the spit
of bewilderment, of overpowering visions—the gods
throw their heads back and they
laugh and laugh, they laugh and they
laugh, until they are rolling on the floor
of the heavenly TV lounge

Poem for Jack Kerouac in California

You hear that dead man
rave and blow, down under
the ground, where form
gets wild and it's like Steve
Carlton plunging his arms into
buckets of uncooked rice
and working his fingers around
to get the power up
through his muscles into the
tendons of his neck and
shoulders and what have you
the bigger the digger
the deeper the grave

Jazz for Jack (April 5, 1949)

Clarence 'Cootie' Williams was a
big shoulder man from Mobile
blew hot trumpet for the Duke
many years, had his own group too
w/ Bud Powell during wartime
recorded 'House of Joy' 'Gator Tail'
wildly swinging sides for Capitol
c. 1943-1944 (w/ Willis Jackson
on tenor
   braying woman-mad
all night balls
    that gassed
Jack Kerouac at 25
    and led
that boy down
    muddy alleys
of the mind
    cross creaking beds
in shacks of honk
    while Memphis Trains
blast thru world nights
  to pour out that hot come
and joy and tears
    in pools
on starlit banks
    and brews
of Saturday Night
     'I'm pulled
out of my shoes
    by wild
stuff like that—
    pure whiskey'

scribbling these notes
on a Saturday night
in the last chance saloon
of life
          where it's
'really our last chance
to be honest'

                    Kerouac
hits the city
again, cuts down
to that neon-lit
crazy jazz shack
of the night
               little notebook
in shirt pocket
                    'I like
Saturday night in the shack
to be crazy
          I like things to GO
and rock and be flipped
I want to be stoned
If I'm going to be stoned at all'

Life is combustion
everybody's a small blue flame
that doesn't mean it doesn't hurt,

a small bunsen burner flame
jewel point
like a gas jet
of dry lunacy
with an orange halo
like a fuzzy chrysanthemum,
yay,

166

and this is the night
in America
and what it does to you

the night does things like that
it makes you burn too fast
you lose all that heat, you crash
on the floor of Clellon Holmes' pad
wake up bugged, like in a blue
zone, w/ sullen yet curious pout
eyes down however — *out* — nothing happening
later shambling w/ serious thoughtful frown
handspockets under sunday trees like in Proust
tho only on gray alien US streets, you stroll
to the subway
and fly home to Long Island like a quiet ghost
just before the Birth of the Cool
and preparing the arrival of the long and coruscating line.

Ted

Choking on la phlegm fatale
malady of the moralist obsessed
by art-as-words-as-life
Though you outsurvived Kerouac
by several months' tenure
on the planet you died the same death
internal combustion of the blood—
Jack, your great hero (along with Frank)—
whom, in your sole encounter,
you appeased with obetrols,
an interview, and reading of "Tambourine Life."
"Get your teeth fixed," Kerouac told you.
When you departed (you later recalled)
Jack looked sad, because you were
"taking all the energy out of the room"
& that's how we feel now.

*

"Just like the old days, only
we are crazier than ever
and more parts ache, too!
I have a sore leg, backache,
my radiator's thermostat seems
busted, and my wheels
are less than rims now.
Still, the mail must go
through! But where did all
these fucking Indians come from?"

—T.B., letter, 18 Dec. '81

*

168

The phone rings & you're dead.
"Put it on the cuff," you used to say, riding by;
"go now, pay later."
Now it's later & the bills are all paid.
You told me many things
useful to the management of the heart
& mind
      tho there toward the end
things got too retrospective
to be behavioral; & finally
I got 2 messages from you
out of that period of which
you told Simon Pettet "wearily,"
"last year was the worst."
The second was: "the pentagon
still hates you, but you are
a major in the army of the young,"
& the first was: "dear tommy: love
spurs us on, you & me, to
only one death. that is why
you can just call me 'laura.' "

                *

What to do when the day's heavy heart
produces baffling combustions everywhere
southwest lost doubloons rest in memory
& the best of urban voices gone

                In memoriam Ted Berrigan
                d. July 4, 1983

The Death of Bop

Plip by plip
strict dribbles of wasted smoop
accumulate into trickles
that wet the beaks of parched tributaries only slightly
Bud Powell died in 1966
with a cigarette still hanging from his lips
and from that point on
the long, coruscating lines that leap and dart with dry lunacy
have been hard to find

The Retirement of Superman

Shivering once and
wrapping my red and blue cloak tightly around myself
I traveled to a rare and terraced land
where there were trees of alabaster
in forests of blasted gold
under petrochemical dawns
I goofed and dreamed, life was very great
human beings didn't need me any more
I received a monthly stipend of 720 free hours
whenever I got hungry all I had to to
was drop my head down
into the submarine dollar ferns of heaven
and chew

The Gray Myth of the West

The tunnel is the eye of a needle.
The light at the end of the tunnel is
caused by the miniature railroad
train of the future bearing down on
us with incredible fission. Casey
Jones is clutching the throttle with
a skeletal hand. Hot cinders
spark and sizzle his nose hairs.
Ahead lie the killing labors of
the Modoc Grade. But Casey
Jones is not afraid. His foot
is attached to the dead man's pedal
by bandages of destiny. Nothing
can halt this continually arriving train
nor widen its rapidly narrowing
gauge. Casey fires up his Camel and rides.

Requiem

for Paula von Wiedersehen

Paula, stay dead. Your life came as a
surprise to us, as life itself does
to a chair made of Bavarian oak. Dying,
you give us hope of a freedom whence
we will gaze back on this pathetic society
like a parent upon disappointing offspring.
It is insubstantial, however, this foothold
which keeps slipping out from under us
every time you unfold the map. Life is
like a cliff upheld by gravel
as rivers of death meander
through it, leaving painted cardboard
canyons. Gravity, in rivers, defies
resistance, as daily life overcomes
the grief of your Endarkenment,
lowering our consciousness. The path
to martyrdom lies through bushes
of ulterior motive beyond which
Love Avoidance crops up, squat
and blossoming with charcoal
lumps. Be devious and manipulative
in order to negotiate the difficult
enfilades of keeping score. Be
sure to project into the future &
demand proofs of love; you will
swim across dry creeks of how
hard you're working, thus balancing
unequal things up. Develop a
negative concept of what

constitutes good sex and avoid it
like a derelict whom you'd hit with your crutch
of little white lies, causing him to fall back
into Virtue, Pride and Self
Sacrifice. Resist your body and its
natural compulsions. Become as
tense as possible. Lock your knees, Paula.
Keep climbing. Suck in your belly.
Make your buttocks very tight.
Keep your breathing as light
as possible. Don't look up. The rocks
feel cold and clammy on your
dead hands. Keep climbing, Paula.
The higher you go the lower you
come. You are an adept endarkener.
You are entering the low places
of always trying to do what's
right. You brag about the dent in
the Cadillac that led your funeral
cortege. You tell us you've been
out dancing the dance of
the dead three nights in a
row. Your negative bragging shows
us the way. Your expressions
of suffering are a tic-tac-toe
of unhappiness that serves as
our guide. We understand you
completely. The gravity of your
left handed compliments, your
disdainful stance and distancing
posture, are all irresistible
and intolerable. You teach us to
avoid all feelings and sensations
and this is what we must do if
we are to follow your rules of thumb.

Avoiding love is the only way out of life
blocking clumps of death that loom
up along the keep busy and work hard
trail. Forget all past successes.
Be somewhere in the strip of your
existence, a very narrow strip
that skirts the edge of an abyss
of blaming. True dark onwardness
flashes up from below. Take on more
than you can manage. The vivid
Sunrise is hidden from us by your freedom
from liberty. Our life's work
is to climb up the step that leads
down into your death.
This is your life. Stay dead
a while. We sing you this soft
wooing song while you roll
over in your tomb unbearably.

Robert Lowell

Was born under the shadow of the Dome of the Boston State House
Was a Pisces
Was born on March 1, worst-fated of birthdays
Came from a family of bankers and Harvard presidents, though his
    father was a naval man
Hated his mother
Was a loner at school
Was called Caliban there, later shortened to "Cal"
Read the Bible, Homer, Shakespeare, Wordsworth & Keats
Ate health food on Nantucket
Hated Harvard
Carried a suitcase of poetry to Nashville to live on Allen Tate's lawn
    in a Sears Roebuck tent
Followed Ford Madox Ford to Boulder
And John Crowe Ransom to Kenyon
Refused to be inducted in the armed forces in 1943
Wrote a letter to President Roosevelt stating his crisis of conscience
22 years later wrote a similar letter to Lyndon Johnson
Protesting America's presence in Vietnam
In between wrote many tight, fist-like, self-revealing poems
Eventually went mad
Wrote to Theodore Roethke that their generation of poets had "a
    flaw in the motor"
Talked often about Hitler and the Blessed Virgin
Created much strain for each of his three wives
Repeatedly renounced his past and announced he was beginning a
    new life
Died

Mark Fidrych

Nobody ever rode a higher wave or gave us more
                                                back of what it taught
Or thought less of it,
Shrugging off the fame it
                                    brought, calling it "no big deal"
And, once it was taken
                            away, refusing bitterness with such
Amazing grace.
Absence of damage limits one's perception
                                                        of existence.
Suffering, while not to be pursued,
Yields at least what Mark
                                    termed "trains of thought,"
Those late, sad milk runs to Evansville
                                                and Pawtucket
Which he viewed
                        not simply as pilgrimages
Of loss, but as interesting trips
In themselves — tickets to ride
                                    that long dark tunnel through
Which everybody — even those less gifted — must sooner
Or later pass
Because, "hey, that's what you call life."

Life is a jungle
The overburdened Herzog
found out the hardware
weighs as much as the
memorial flowers

Dark as Day

As when the god-hammered payne's gray
naval armada of clouds rolls its slow
length along the goleta valley, moving east,
massing to deliver another pulse of low,
low pressure, with gulps and bolts
of rain, so also the weather builds
in the human psyche, where storms of act
move in with frequency and cause pain,
bringing about a new understanding of
the natural history of the soul: too
late though for the 40,000 breathers who lost
theirs last night: it's like life's a school
they're today's graduating class
perhaps to be kept alive on the space shuttle to Utah
inside the first orbital bio-feedback cardiac agony prolonger
they say only one or two unlucky arrivals will be chosen to
        volunteer
meanwhile the sky keeps getting darker and rain
at last unravels the ink-stained cloud diplomas

Somewhere in the West—
A Riddle

The closer the bone the sweeter the bite:
Among dark thoughts of slips between
Cups and lips, afternoon meets night
In the shadowed Hopper picture window

(Shrouded in analgesic light)
Which the woman in the white traveling dress
Traverses, nervous, with red tortoiseshell shades.
She stops to consider coffee.

She kills her cigarette and raises
To her red lips a man's black china mug
Emblazoned, in a bow-tie lariat script,
"No Regrets," by decal. The motel dims

Into the perfidy of saffron electrical dusk
With the entry of a second figure,
A hatless man in a plain dark suit
Who does something mysterious with his hands.

Emotional balances perceptibly shift
At this point, like the inside parts of a lock
Coaxed toward their decision. He bends.
She goes back across the room again

Making snowy egrets glide
Under her. Do these people know
They are part of a story that tumbles
Abruptly forward now, pitching

Them forty-two years into a future
That is framed on the wall of memory's sad
Museum? Night, the light-rustler,
Comes on in a soft crushing agitation

Of blue neon fruit against the
Cadmium orange sky. What
Goes up must come down.
But who are they? Why were they born?

Entropical Question

Is the universe nostalgic about itself
as it runs down
or is entropy an essentially
unsentimental process
I believe the latter
and all around I see
a vizine synapse
as beautiful as a sunset in baja
eyes drying in the wash
of decaying detail

Epitaph

The sun goes down again in appalling dusty
beauty over the distances and reaches
of a landscape toward which men seldom did
feel anything but an earnest greed
a hand over fist desire to acquire

space, the currency of time, later recognized
(but only too late) to be exhaustible

Early Warning

> *My books have done me more harm than*
> *anything else! . . . 'never write' . . .*
> *that's the big thing!*
> —Céline

1

The full moon shines on the killing floor
chilling the will to live until morning
a spill of color to outlast the lightfall
dim mutinous audibilities shifting
like fingers lifting single strings letting
them fall again, a billion millilinguals mingling
hybrid voices of izquierdo lillywhite
vacillation and assault until left
for dead in the derecho gaucho gauze.
Inchling sun swims slightly higher,
slides back down.

2

Seeing Klaus Kinski as Aguirre on his raft
shook me the way an unmistakable craft
metaphor always provides a really
shocking early warning of what lies
ahead, downstream, miles of fearful
river still to be traversed, *en*
voyage into the terrible interior
of the soul, where to go crazy
is the least of the imminent dangers
and to get off the boat alive is
not one of the more realistic hopes

3

Events leave me convinced
whoever it was devised
the game of existence
was very wise to place
right next to the bright
and noisome ego, that
dark and silent drive
the instinct for death. This
black zone takes the position
of the zero in roulette.
The Casino always wins.

4

They say Charon the boatman plies his oar
inside the tiniest burst arteriole
just like a ship placed inside a bottle
his craft can negotiate passages
so small, simply to consider
the beauty of such navigation assuages
the sense of justice, elsewise unconsoled
in this technomedical age ("I'll get out alive!")
which assumes the drowner dodges
the swinging bluntness of the rudder:
a chance equal to that of a wave avoiding the shore

5

Hey Mr. Handsome, shoot *this* with your Minolta!
Boy, will you look funny in Charon's sampan
Ugly mug split in half from ear to ear
Once he's flailed his big oaken rudder
Upside that map you used to find so pretty
When you pondered it in the hand mirror
Which was the same one you also employed as a deck
To divide up those rocks of pure brain candy
So you could blow them up your neck
And induce a flashdunce inside your brainpan
That let you out-stupid even John Travolta

6

Berchtesgaden-among-the-palms
Larry Speakes, in tropical sportshirt
wants to talk about the spacewalkers
w/ their toy buck rogers backpacks
but wont touch hot potato questions
from uppity press corps hodads
asking how come the 16 inch guns
of the new jersey are busting not
"syrian positions" but druze villages
what if those villages were in israel?
then who'd pay for these charades?

7

Lying up here on the roof amid the spanish tiles
flat on my back with a sore throat
staring up thru oak branches into the azure
holding the FM antenna over my head w/ one hand
so Bach harpsichord concerto can make it
all the way from KPFK in LA here to the foothills
of Mission Canyon through the constant static
induced by ten-to-the-hour mass overflights
of military choppers hauling SS men to and from
the currently occupied Presidential ranch
who ever said beauty came easy?

8

All senses of efficiency
and competence are false.
Nothing is free in this world. Sooner
or later everything's paid for
not only things done badly
but things done well. The latter
cost a good deal more.
Isn't that only natural? From
the carefully designed elevation
of a sense of material perfection
it's a much longer fall.

9

Fifty books down the line I find
two of them still in print
every now & then some uninformed
or stubborn person manages
to discover my early works
stacked in dusty cold storage
under a pyramid of returns
from which probably just fate
the unexpectedly retrieved
text utters a nearly audible
grumble, like an interrupted sleeper's

10

There might be a future for you in the wax museum
said the curator, if you learn how to shut your mouth
and stop offending our prospective customers
who knows, some day a historical tendency
might turn left and run through your asshole
weirder things have happened, I can't think of one
offhand but if you give me two or three years . . .
and by the way, what did you say your name was?
hey, where you going, what's your hurry?
if you take that attitude, there's nothing we
can do for you . . . you didn't have to slam the door!

11

Homo deliquensis, or faces in a crowd
turtle, parakeet, jackass—I've lost the human touch!
there goes someone who not only looks
like a dog, but is followed by one
no longer can I summon up
a feeling of relationship with this race of mutants
by which I'm involuntarily surrounded
I've got 2 wheels on my bicycle
and three toes on one foot
I keep getting the feeling something essential's
missing but I don't know what

12

To drag Death around like a doppelgänger, stiff
with knee braces and orthotic inserts, or to stare
Him in the puss—"part ape part tiger"—either way
there's no avoiding mortality's basic factness
which lurks in back of every tactically-evasive
fiction. This said, cheer up! Mr. D's only
a white version of Mr. T: "Ah likes to, uh, beat
people up!" Bullies are easy to tease. This
is a source of comedy, one of life's few serious
pleasures. At the mouth of the cave the half-blind beast appears,
scratching himself. You scream "sissy!" and split, limping.

13

The one thing that's ever
interested me in the training
of Tibetan lamas is the
rubric about going through
various increasingly painful
ordeals, until one reaches
that stage of wisdom where
one no longer says anything
at all—the stage at which
one is, at long last,
left completely alone.

14

Life's unfortunately complicated
by the prevailing assumption that
happiness is some kind of big deal
and the corollary supposition
it should be attained. The upshot of
this general social delusion
is a universal sense of private
disappointment, which might easily
be avoided if people realized
life's ideal equation is not
kicks^2 times one but zero minus pain.

15

The buoyancy of a trilling flute floating
atop a celestial passage of Handel
performed by the great orchestra in
the sky is almost enough to drown out
barking dogs and crosstown traffic but
not quite. Readjusting the headphones
I see my wife's pleasant face rising up
over the top rung of the ladder exactly
at roof level. Just as she speaks a bird
twitters in the green oak above her head.
I make a silent vow never to complain about life again.

16

And then a certain heavenly screaming *d'amore*
envelops me and drives me into a cosmic unison
momentarily. I hope it goes away soon
because it's too confusing. It does. Great applause
follows, hectic violins and a contest of bluejays
for space in the oak branches. Territorial displays
are stated. The soprano broaches a lament. Dolors
are reiterated by harpsichords but only delicately
and then there is a rising feeling of *mirabile*
that catches hold, swells, explodes into joyous
emotion such as has been all but unknown locally.

17

And now a crow upon the telephone
pole exploits the noonday stillness
to break into great claims of precedence.
The mission bells toll. A breeze comes
up and moves around in the sky blue I LOVE
LIFE/ LIVE AND LET LIVE t-shirt
that's draped across the red tiles to dry.
Faint cirrus drifts by like divine laundry.
Smooth as cream the contralto states
her case for the heart's somber
glory. Love gleams out across *l'universo.*

18

There's a certain passion in the absence
of passion. What's not busy may still move
with great concerted emotion. Force
looms up like undersea currents from the
cellos. A tentative vibrato replies in
the slow building of an argument which
develops inch by inch and millimeter
by millimeter, like a starfish crossing
the ocean floor. Suddenly, *presto!* soar
the fingers of light across an undisturbed
surface. Calmly Neptune awakens.

19

The bride's rescued from decapitation by sarazens
inside Handel's amazing brain; it was the desert,
all the time, not the ocean, upon
which this incredible action was taking
place. Cool colors and shades of violet
with silver scrollwork, moorish muslin,
great plumed helmets and fine gold
embroidery were worn but I did not need
to see them: the entire experience took
place inside my imagination. But I'm not tempted
to let it go to my head. I no longer have one!

20

Handel stole the plot of this baroque opera
from ol' Torquato Tasso. How'd it go?
Godfrey of Boulogne leads the christian army
through a kind of *déjà vu* during, what,
the first crusade? Kidnapings, slayings,
alliances, aragon: in this tale of jerusalem
prophetically forecast five centuries
ago, nothing's missing but the shi'ite militia
and larry speakes lying about it all
under the fortune palms; the baritone booms
just like the big guns of the new jersey.

21

The careful distribution of energy and relaxation
occurs like clockwork inside woodwinds and violins.
Gales and hurricanes lend wings to the feet. But
a change of heart is the central event, not only
in Tasso's poem but also in Handel's opera
and even, perhaps, in this calloused listener
who finds himself suddenly rapt by vocalizations
in a language he only haltingly
understands. The point however is not the words
which may move the mind, but the music
which moves feelings long since unmoved.

22

Jubilation is not something to be found inside
the bell of a trumpet, even if you get a
stiff neck looking for it. Near a bay, a ship
lies moored. Mermaids play in the water.
One combs her long hair. She sings to Renaldo.
It is Maytime. In his heart the sap rises.
He vows to overcome all obstacles. But fate
is cruel. There will be treachery and weeping.
Many challenges must be met with true
courage, but gentleness must not be forgot,
and at the end all will be lost, save the lamenting.

23

Persephone wades ashore, droplets still
sparkling in her hair like a wet tiara.
It has been a long swim in the underworld.
She shed her bikini unconsciously on
the rocks, it's long since lost, she's
forgotten about it. Her skin has an olive
darkness through which a pearly lustre
glows. Which way to the *albergo?*
The mermaids wave toward the village, then giggle
lightly as she walks languidly away,
the shed drops drying into diamonds behind her.

24

Renaldo has never seen anything like her
during all those years of fighting against
the sarazens, lances, anger, blood.
Dumbstruck, he hides behind a garden wall
until she's gone past, then trails
her as far as the local trattoria, where
she again stops to ask directions. He's
aching to leap out and inform her
the only hotel in town's famous for its lice
and his ship's really a lot more comfortable.
But the poor lad, long on hope, is short on nerve.

25

How did a girl like her get into an opera
like this one? Wrong story, wrong century, wrong
everything. Renaldo can't sort it out.
He's still scratching his head when the curtain
comes down on act two. We see him erring
through the town, downcast, a chianti
bottle hooked on his index finger.
Persephone registers at the hotel, makes
a couple of phone calls, takes a shower
(no hot water, alas!), then hits the sack. Renaldo
stands under her window, thinking, wondering.

26

A wind rises in the east, and from the hill
on which the village is situated
one can see a fleet of galleons making
for the harbor under full sail.
It's the main expeditionary force,
on its way to engage the sarazens.
Dio mio, says Renaldo to himself,
mama mia! What a time
for a bloody crusade! I've
got better things to do! Think I'll
take a rain check this time around!

27

He hides out in the hotel cellar
for two weeks, eating acorns
smuggled to him by shepherds
and sneaking out every morning
for a glance at Persephone
when she comes out on her balcony
to yawn and stretch and greet
the day. It isn't much but it's better
than nothing, and the fleet puts
out to sea without him. I'm worth no more
than a dog! he thinks, but at least I'm breathing.

28

Finally one sultry evening Persephone descends
to the cellar in search of a
cool spot to sit and think; she's
got serious things on her mind,
things Renaldo wouldn't have
dreamed of. Taking his heart in
his hands, he confronts her there.
She smiles. He melts into a puddle
of liquid ex-crusader before her
on the cool cellar floor; before
he can pull himself together, she vanishes.

29

The strings continue to tremble and vibrate
in a continuing expression of feelings
Renaldo could articulate in no other
way; but even the marvelous music
cannot explain exactly what is in
his heart, which he is certain must
be broken. This apparition of a girl
has checked out without leaving
a forwarding address. Renaldo drifts
aimlessly down to the waterfront,
where the brainless mermaids console him.

30

The crusaders return. Our hero re-enlists,
and no questions are asked. Soon
the fleet embarks again, and Renaldo
finds himself in the midst of the battle
for Jerusalem. Steel flashing, great
bursts of crimson, enormous male
yells and the rearings of huge
horses are all Renaldo knows for
the next several weeks. The Sarazen
is defeated, but as everyone realizes, will
rise up again fearlessly next season.

31

Like the rest of us, this young man whose
all-too-human behavior has been
transformed into poetry by Tasso
and thence into great music by
Handel and thence back into
a very different kind of sea-changed
narrative by yours truly, is
subject to sudden mutations of
intention that alter everything
he does, and render him therefore
stubbornly resistant to "programming."

32

And isn't it programming, really,
which makes the modern world,
with its android-citizens moving
digitally along temperature-controlled
circuit diagrams, so uniquely
hard to take? Or am I missing
something essential in contemporary
life, something which I should be
not only able but ready and
willing and even eager to like and
enjoy? Is lack of soul really a serious omission?

33

Is this just the reflexive grumbling of a
cripple? Am I barking up the wrong tree
by identifying too much with Renaldo?
Are these mutants I think I'm encircled by
real, or only figments of my disordered
imagination? Am I climbing a celestial
ladder made out of pieces of cloud
or does this eighteenth century music
really conduct me to literal realms of
absolutely clear vision, whence the present
looks much less substantial than dreams?

34

A blast of brass outside the walls
of Jerusalem. Angels rush in
where fools fear to tread. Great
clashes of vocalized emotion
create waves and crests of thought
that has no "referential" sense
at all. That doesn't mean it has
no sense. In a thousand years
no one on earth will speak Italian
but if there's anyone left on earth
at all, this music will still yield feeling.

What human brain in bondage to technology
could rise to this precision of ecstasy
created two centuries ago by Handel?
Who ever programmed a machine to leap
outside the material world with such
extreme elasticity of joy! O tell
me, Muse, what lingo-poop mumbling
into his lectern could pretend to shoot
out into the heavens with excitement
of mind and heart equal to this! I say
have mercy! Forget it! Take a break!

36

The old stories are still the best ones
Going from one country into another through
a thousand terrible adventures, oh my!
Ferocious armies! thundering from the sky
and the sea! Blasting and roasting! Men
and armored trains, burning babes, mothers
in law tied to the rails! Flying fortresses
roaring! Whole squadrons of men butchered by
the sarazens while the french horns blare!
Flares and tracers! Deluges of blood! Fireworks
and Grand Guignol! Flames! Bombs! Belfries!

37

Fire pots! Tremolos! Speeches! All of
Europe toasted like a marshmallow on a fork!
America in ruins! Nuclear holocaust! Long
winters of Armageddon! Give me wars
O goddess! Send phosphor fires O muse!
Explode cities in front of my eyes! Let me hear
the cries of whole nations rising up in suffering!
Blow the universe out your ass! Let the whole
shithouse go up in radioactive smoke! See
if I care! What's here worth saving?
Anything the scholars of infinity might miss?

38

Or maybe you'd prefer something a little quieter
than war, maybe a nice silent inhaled pesticide
bearing the specific carcinogen that will mate with
a certain potential oncogene in your esophagus?
Just another figment of my imagination, or sign
of things to come? A precise little appetizer,
fibroma, tumor of the bronchial passage, the tongue?
An epithelioma or two? Something sweet and exact
just north of the pharynx? Closure of the breathing tube?
Stomach lining? Prostate? Colon? Lung? You won't have to
wait too long, it's probably already gaining on you.

39

Kentucky Fried Chicken, go ahead, chow down,
munch munch, McDonald's, Wimpy's, Denny's
beef burned in grease, PCB, cholesterol, sodium,
asbestos, EDB, cooking oil, fat, sizzling
frying, dripping, broiling, phew! Have another one!
Go ahead! Beer scotch wine and brandy! Champagne!
Vodka! Puff puff! Cigarette, pipe, cigar! Cocaine!
Why stop now! Salami! Bacon! Butter!
Rot! Swill! Die! Rub up to the bumper!
Snout down to the trough! Myocarditis! Taco Bell!
Arteriosclerosis! Cancer! Sushi! Coffin stuffing!

40

Faith healers! Est squadrons! Neo-Tibetans!
Diet crackpots! Self visualizers! Holistic creeps!
Aerobic meditators! Joggers! Nautiloids!
Eraserheads! Leg warmers! Jazz dancers! Happy-face freaks!
Nobody gets out alive, not even if they interact!
Not the programmers, not even the user-friendlies,
not even the consultants, the analysts, the arts
administrators! The white-collars! The grant
writers! Sheep-coordinators! Fakers! Smilers!
Doctor Feelgoods! Steroid gulpers! Space walkers!
Video watchers! Born again! Forever young!

41

I'm not very long on confidence, I don't have
confidence in anything! Not in myself! In you!
In this poem! But what I do have confidence
in is time! Everything keeps on going
and covers up everything else that came before!
Everything is forgotten! History is the last
few drops in the bucket! Folks who lived
in caves in the alluvial deltas of
Southern Europe probably remembered things
nobody's ever heard of today! A million years
from now nobody will remember this! And that's good!

42

The whole crowd of poetry clones rushes me
They lynch me, tear me to pieces!
Right here in the middle of my poem!
Every bone in my body smashed to jelly!
Femur! Skull! Pelvis! Eyes gouged out!
Face bashed open with a hammer!
Brains running out through my ears!
Disemboweled belly leaking tripe!
Vomiting blood all over! Apologize!
They want me to apologize before I'm allowed
To kick the bucket! But no! I won't! Too bad!

43

Driven together by a desire to contend
Knowing no life but that of rivalry
They continued to buy and sell each other's souls
Even in this enclave of fugitives
Though allegedly they were dedicated to poetry
Instead it was envy that motivated them
So that they resembled rabid dogs
Traveling in a pack with maximum infighting
The attention of the group turned instantly to any
Renegade who threatened to outdistance
The rest, and this outlaw was collectively attacked

44

Mutual reinforcement's the name of the game
to survive in the "arts" you've got to be a belonger
if not to a school, then to a club,
a cell, a lodge, a party, a police force
only the party standard bearers
are awarded the laurels of the party
all non-belongers are branded "paranoid" —
distrustful, dangerously suspicious (i.e., wise
to the condition of being outsiders); I'm
(for instance) as ingenuous and naively trusting
as your average Sudanese mercenary killer

45

There is no interpretation necessary.
You got to deal with the man the way
the man going to deal with you. No hate
but to relate to history not forgetting
the mistake of those who'd evade it. Sticks
and stones will certainly break my brittle
bones but the stunted drone of the many
poetry clones only makes me laugh and study
ways to gain a new power over words
that are so stubborn, to steer them into clear
and simple sentences is a good lifetime's work.

46

Copper, iron, lead, graphite, phosphate, zinc . . .
Palm oil is used for margarine, soap,
lubrication. The ground nut and cola nut
produce oils. Cotton becomes flax.
Export of coffee, grains, fabrics, oil, gold,
rubber, fruits, this is the story of
colonialism in Africa. The story of
human labor turned into money for distant
people to create pyramids of power
in banks is the story of Europe. This
is where we got the language we use.

47

I got the blood that flows in me
from dirt ireland, factory england, and indians
that didn't know how to sue
the government. The industrial world
gave us the computer world we employ
today. Uranium, radium, tin, iron,
spices. Diamonds. Food for thought.
It all came from somewhere. You can't
give anything back but you can stop
taking it. Start making and using it.
Only if you get the sentences clear.

It's got to start somewhere and where
it might start is to stop letting
the government guide the publishing
by dumping money in the liar hopper,
to spin the liar wheels in the monkey
see monkey do literary biz which is
really only exploitation of paper to
perpetrate the lie that wanting to be
an artist is equal to being one. For that
way lies the spreading fog of unclear
speech. Big business can use that for a pillow.

Personal items of use to white people include
such artifacts as books which create
the pressure of babble against silence.
Silence which is at least pure like
a nuclear blast. This is clear. To arouse
the race with thought and action is a higher
way. Only clear speech which comes from
language in contact with emotion
and thought can spread the truth that brings
the pyramid of power down to pieces on
the ground. Splice this into what is happening.

50

Charon rows around in the obscurantists' heads
under cover of the darkness and fog of
death which is their misuse of language
he bashes the 2000 billion neurons each
with an individual blast of his heavy oar
wham! pieces of cerebrum all over
the place, big waves of neural mutation
splashing up against the sides of
the cranium, horrible bruising, scars,
hematomas, he skims off their thoughts
and knocks loose the faulty synaptic connections

51

"Waking them up," he calls this forcible
stirring of the neural jelly
which is really a service to the human race
because it takes place at the midnight
hour, the time of gross communication-decay,
the age of linguistic collapse, when speech
has been reduced to idiot mumbles
meaningless except to fellow perpetrators
of the mass atrocity against sense—
you might even say that by performing this service
old Charon is operating as a kind of cultural Red Cross

52

You know if you've been through it
You can't stand it any more
You're up to your neck in horror
You're ready to take a few chances
Step on a few toes
To have been born somewhere else
Or not born at all
Those are celestial thoughts aren't they?
Death, okay, but no more of this
You just crawl back into the magnet
There's absolutely no reasoning involved

53

Sometimes inside myself I sense
A monstrous insect evolving
Toward some cataclysmic birth
Like the cosmic scene at the beginning
of *Eraserhead* — I'm only
Telling you this because it's fair
To give you early warning
That some not too distant day
You might step outside your house
And find a whole species like me
Crawling out of their husks toward you

54

What's called my life is
Just my own peculiar
Way of jumping the gun
On death
Look closely
You'll see the skull
Leering at you through the face
And the skeleton
Poking out in broken pieces
Like the scaffolding of a burntout building
Through the skin

55

We're all going to take
The same train
Sometime before very long
Regardless of age or social standing
It'll pull into your station
You'll get on board
It'll pull out
You'll think it's going to stop
At this town or that one
But the truth is, once underway
It becomes an express

56

The Federico García Lorchestra of my dreams
produces conjunctions beyond the ken of binary
digital calculation but so does yours, therefore
the whole subject's really not worth the serious interest
of an adult. Presumably we're all adults here.
Your average Sudanese mercenary killer has
dreams that probably resemble mine and yours.
The minute he begins to describe them we both fall
asleep and the snoring can be heard in San Francisco.
Everything that is of no interest can be heard
in San Francisco. Presumably this problem is serious.

57

Jack Spicer came and went. Walt Whitman
came. Federico García Lorca went. Johanna
Went was here. Kilroy came and went. Roi
Jones went and Amiri Baraka came. Marilyn
Monroe came. The great existence railway station of going
and coming is as busy now as it ever was.
Everything is always the same as it ever was
but nothing lasts. Everything disappears.
Persephone disappears. Renaldo comes and goes.
Tom Clark comes and goes. Louis-Ferdinand
Destouches comes and goes in my brain, immortal.

58

New graffiti on Atascadero bikeway:
"His Possessions Multiplied and He Began
To Suffocate." "Jesus Died for You." "Death
Before Disco." "Reagan Acted His Way
Into The White House." And this month's winner:
"They Cloned Hitler's Cock!" Lock bike, walk slowly
up seven floors, sit amid comatose
young christians in glass booth, read *Romans*
of Céline, Vol. II, watch the silvery tints
change out on the gray water. "I used to be
pitiful, but not any more. Now I'm indifferent."

59

"An immense hatred keeps me alive." That's Céline.
"I have spent my time putting myself in desperate
situations." A writer's life. This isn't about bullfights.
Glamor? Walter Mitty? "I don't live. I don't exist."
"I used to be pitiful, but not any more. Now I'm
indifferent." What other way to write? You say it's easy?
"It looks like nothing at all but it takes know-how."
Try telling Barry Watten. Happiness? "By myself on the
        seashore,
no one to bother me." No writer ever got there. "Fate towers
so high above us, the squall carries us off like fleas in the
        water . . ."
"Death is only a cleaning machine . . ."

A true writer's a mere work tool
Whose job is to efface
All traces of his labor
With such thoroughness and care
That the reader may without knowing it
Experience in every line
A lifetime's curiosity and pain
Squeezed down by sheer hard work
Into that glorious product commonly dismissed
By referring to it with the ultimately
Patronizing term Style

It's only typical that
the week of the death of
the greatest modern french writer
and one of the century's few really honest men
who dropped dead in mid-sentence while still writing brilliantly
the cover of paris-match was a portrait
not of this man céline
but of a very famous bullshitter
who'd blown his brains out in an american ski resort
because he was no longer able to write a single truthful line

62

Céline brought writing closer to the nerves.
He got on everybody's nerves. Being
a pain in the ass in writing has certain
obvious advantages. A pain in the
ass is rarely boring. It takes nerve
to forego making yourself attractive
to your readers. It also moves you
much deeper into your readers' lives.
No one ever read Céline's books as a
sedative. The reader is either exalted
or annoyed but he is definitely awake.

63

People are afraid of two things they don't
understand, ideas and death. Which is
more dangerous? Who can say? Probably
the former. The fear of death often
contributes to useful behavioral reforms
whereas the fear of ideas is a source
of a great deal of useless behavior. Of course
by "death" I mean the painful extinction of ego, not simple
non-being (which is the same thing as heaven) and by "ideas"
I don't mean what passes for same here in the library.

64

No doubt the most dangerous
thoughts one can harbor
are those which are literally
unspeakable. Until these
quite terrible things have
finally been ejected into
the world by being uttered
the difficulty will continue.
But once they are spoken
the fear of silence will end
and we'll be able to shut up.

65

My days of running off at the mouth are behind me
I don't have anybody left to shoot the shit with
except my wife, who tends to wonder
what she ever did to deserve these exchanges —
and certain dead men, who mind
much less because theirs is
such a silent realm, and any words we manage
come as welcome when
a quiet eternity's the only
alternative: in fact some of them
(like ted) seem never to get enough of these talks

66

The poem is slowing down and losing
its anger and starting to move toward
a certain stasis which means it's almost time
to go. I'm up here on the roof again in
the local color. An ancient Mississippi
Blues kind of koto music's going on
in the headphones and on the porch of
the red house a little girl's saying
"I gave it to that cat!" All the thoughts
I thought I had have gone and that
leaves only thin air and this kind of light feeling.

Printed April 1984 in Santa Barbara &
Ann Arbor for the Black Sparrow Press by
Graham Mackintosh & Edwards Brothers Inc.
Design by Barbara Martin. This edition is
published in paper wrappers; there are 200
cloth trade copies; 200 hardcover copies are
numbered & signed by the author; & 26
lettered copies have been handbound in boards
by Earle Gray, each with an original drawing
by Tom Clark.

TOM CLARK, the author of this personal field guide to the contemporary West, was born in Chicago in 1941 and has since lived all over the U.S. and in Europe. Since 1968 he and his wife and daughter have resided for various periods in northern California, southern Californa, and Colorado. Clark is a graduate of the University of Michigan, attended Cambridge University on a Fulbright, later taught poetry in England and the U.S., served for ten years as *The Paris Review*'s poetry editor, and wrote numerous volumes of poetry, four novels, two books on baseball, and three biographies (of Damon Runyon, Mark Fidrych and Jack Kerouac). He has also worked as a journalist, and is currently a book reviewer for several newspapers, including the *San Francisco Chronicle* and *Los Angeles Herald Examiner*. His art work has been shown in several exhibitions. Clark's books include *When Things Get Tough on Easy Street: Selected Poems 1963–1978* (1978), and *The Last Gas Station and Other Stories* (1980), both published by Black Sparrow Press.